The GIRLS' BOOK of GLAMOUR

A GUIDE TO BEING A GODDESS

Written by Sally Jeffrie
Illustrated by Nellie Ryan
Edited by Liz Scoggins
Designed by Zoe Quayle

The GIRLS' BOOK of GLAMOUR

A GUIDE TO BEING A GODDESS

SCHOLASTIC INC.

New York   Toronto   London   Auckland   Sydney
Mexico City   New Delhi   Hong Kong   Buenos Aires

FOR THE LOVELY KATE JEFFRIE

Library of Congress Cataloging-in-Publication Data

Jeffrie, Sally.
The girls' book of glamour : a guide to being a goddess / written by Sally Jeffrie; illustrated by Nellie Ryan; edited by Liz Scoggins; designed by Zoe Quayle. — 1st American ed.
p. cm.
"First published in Great Britain in 2008 by Buster Books."
ISBN-13: 978-0-545-08537-3
ISBN-10: 0-545-08537-3
1. Preteens — Life skills guides — Juvenile literature. 2. Girls — Life skills guides — Juvenile literature.
3. Etiquette for girls — Juvenile literature. I. Title.
HQ777.J44 2009
646.7'046 — dc22
2008017119

First published in Great Britain in 2008 by Buster Books, an imprint of Michael O'Mara Books Limited, 9 Lion Yard, Tremadoc Road, London SW4 7NQ, United Kingdom

Text and illustrations copyright © Buster Books 2008

Cover design by Angie Allison
(from an original design by www.blacksheep-uk.com)
Cover illustration: Paul Moran

12 11 10 9 8 7 6 5 4 3 2 1   9 10 11 12 13 14/0

Printed in the U.S.A.
First American edition, January 2009

CONTENTS

NOTE TO READERS

The publisher and author disclaim all liability for accidents, injuries, or loss that may occur as a result of information or instructions given in this book.
The most glamorous girls use their best common sense at all times. Be very careful with scissors, needles, kitchen equipment, and hot liquids, and get permission from the appropriate adult before using any tools or utensils. Be mindful of the ingredients noted and your own allergies and medical condition. Stay within the law and local rules, and be considerate of other people.

HOW TO MAKE A GOOD FIRST IMPRESSION

First impressions usually last, so follow these pointers to make everyone's first thoughts of you the best they can be.

- Remember to introduce yourself and ask the other person's name.
- Look the other person in the eye, smile, and remember to speak clearly.
- Pay attention to what the other person is saying.
- Ask questions about his or her interests and hobbies.
- Just be yourself.

HOW TO TAKE A COMPLIMENT

There's nothing like receiving dozens of compliments to build up your confidence, even if you blush with embarrassment at first. It's a good idea to use these tips the next time a friend says something nice about you.

- DO smile and say "thank you."
- DO be modest.
- DO compliment your friend in return.
- DON'T frown, mumble, or look at the floor.
- DON'T just say "I know."
- DON'T disagree.

HOW TO DESCEND A STAIRCASE GRACEFULLY

An important part of glamour is impressing people, and there's no better way to do that than with a grand entrance. Whether you're arriving at a ball or just trying to wow your friends at school, descending a staircase with style and grace can make a great impression. Here are some pointers for making the best entrance ever – and avoiding any embarrassing slips, trips, or falls:

- Pause at the top of the stairs and gaze confidently around the room for a few seconds until everyone turns to look at you.

- Discreetly check the staircase for any obvious hazards or obstacles before you take a step.

- If you are in a long ballgown, make sure you lift up the bottom of your dress so you don't trip.

- Lift up your chin, smile, and then lightly grip the handrail to help you keep your balance.

- Step gracefully down onto the first step, keep smiling, and remember not to look at your feet.

- Walk carefully and steadily down the stairs until you reach the bottom. *Voilà.*

HOW TO FLATTER A FRIEND

An essential part of glamour is making other people feel great about themselves, too. So don't just focus on yourself – add an aura of niceness to your personality. Remember to compliment your friends and classmates on their best qualities and you'll soon see how good it makes them feel about themselves.

THINGS YOU SHOULD SAY

- "Your hair looks lovely."
- "I love your drawings."
- "You're really talented."
- "That really compliments your eyes."
- "You've got really nice handwriting."
- "You're so well coordinated."
- "You're so good at sports."

THINGS YOU SHOULDN'T SAY

- "That's so last season."
- "Get with the program!"
- "You shouldn't wear that color again."
- "What on earth are you wearing?"
- "Ha ha ha ha ha ha."

HOW TO CUSTOMIZE YOUR SCHOOL UNIFORM

It is possible to express your own style even if you have to wear a school uniform. Here's how to do it without risking detention:

- Find out about your school's uniform policy. How much you'll be able to customize your uniform depends on how strict your school is. Don't go too far and risk detention!

- Most schools don't insist you wear a particular size or length – within reason. For instance, if you like loose clothes, then opt for a blazer in a slightly larger size so it hangs in a baggy style.

- If you have to wear a tie, think about how you'll wear it. Perhaps you'd like it very short with a fat knot, or maybe you'd prefer it long with a thin knot. Experiment.

- Check out sales of secondhand school uniforms – most schools have them yearly. Designs of school uniforms subtly change over the years, and you might prefer the vintage style of a secondhand item to the new ones currently being sold.

- Investigate which items you're allowed to choose for yourself and then really express your taste with them. For instance, backpacks can be transformed with a pin or decorative key chain, shoes can be updated by adding colored laces, and a new hairstyle can be created with different barrettes.

- If your school only insists that you wear certain colors rather than specific items of clothing, you're really in luck. You'll be able to experiment with a wide variety of great styles while sticking to the color rule.

Remember — it's definitely your personality and not what you wear that really matters.

HOW TO EAT YOUR WAY TO BEAUTIFUL SKIN

Lotions and potions are great and smell nice, but the very best way to get beautiful skin is from the inside out, which means eating a skin-friendly, healthy diet.

WATER WORKS

You should drink plenty of water throughout the day to keep your skin clear and bright. Aim for about six glasses a day and avoid soda, which is full of sugar.

FRESH AND FRUITY

You should try to eat at least five portions of fresh fruits and vegetables every day. Skin-friendly superfoods include carrots, broccoli, apricots, strawberries, watercress, and oranges. They're great for the rest of your body, too.

GREAT NEWS!

Experts can't find any evidence to link eating chocolate with having problematic skin, so you can still indulge occasionally.

PERFECT DAILY MEAL PLAN

It's important not to skip meals — a regular, healthy diet can work wonders on your skin and will give you lots of energy.

Breakfast. Start with a glass of fresh juice and whole-grain cereal with sliced bananas and milk, followed by toast and honey.

Lunch. Make a cheese or ham sandwich on whole wheat bread with salad followed by yogurt and fruit.

Dinner. Go for grilled chicken and a baked potato with fresh vegetables, followed by fresh fruit salad with yogurt and nuts.

Snacks. Don't go hungry between meals. If you feel cranky, try a healthy snack to keep you going. Fruit, nuts, vegetable sticks, crackers, yogurt, or a slice of whole-grain toast are far better for you than candy or chips.

HOW TO MAKE YOUR OWN LIP GLOSS

To give your lips a delicious glow, you need a great lip gloss. There's no need to spend a fortune, though – it's easy to make your own.

Gather together the following ingredients:

- 2 tablespoons petroleum jelly

- 1 teaspoon honey

- 2 drops extract – peppermint, strawberry, or vanilla are particularly good

- A sprinkle of ultrafine, cosmetic-grade glitter from an arts and crafts store (optional)

Mix all the ingredients together until thoroughly blended. Transfer the mixture to a small, clean pot or jar (with a lid), and apply regularly to your lips for a stunning shine.

HOW TO PUT ON A FASHION SHOW

This is a really glamorous way for you and your friends to spend a rainy afternoon. Get everyone to bring a selection of their favorite clothes, accessories, and jewelry. Then take turns being the stylist, model, and photographer at your own runway show!

You'll need:

- A camera

- A great soundtrack you can strut your stuff to

- Some adults to watch the final show (optional)

THE STYLIST'S JOB

- Select a stunning outfit for your model to wear.

- Chew gum and talk loudly on your cell phone.

- Wear enormous sunglasses while you tell your model what to wear.

THE MODEL'S JOB

- Chew gum, talk on your cell phone, and demand things.

- Look bored while reading an important work of literature.

- Perfect your "model walk." With your head high and your shoulders back, place one foot directly in front of the other as though you're walking on a tightrope.

- Most importantly, never smile.

THE PHOTOGRAPHER'S JOB

- Talk to the model as you take her photograph. Say things like "Love the camera, darling," "That outfit looks divine," and "Look this way, this way – wonderful!"

THE FINAL SHOW

Set up a runway in the living room with chairs or cushions on either side for your audience. Let the audience in, get the music playing, and send your model down the runway while the photographer takes shots of her and the audience applauds wildly.

HOW TO GET THE SHINIEST HAIR EVER

If your hair's looking dull and dirty, it's time to take some action. A few extra treats will soon have it back to its shiny, healthy best.

- **Be a Water Baby.** Just as drinking lots of water can help brighten your skin, a good dose of H_2O can keep your hair shiny, too.

- **Lather up.** If your hair is looking less than glamorous, lather up regularly with a mild shampoo to keep the dirt at bay.

- **Shampoo Dry Hair.** If your hair is ultradirty, try applying the shampoo straight onto dry hair, then leave it in for a couple of minutes before you rinse.

- **Get Conditioning.** Condition your hair regularly to guarantee silky, shiny tresses. Try this easy recipe for a luxurious homemade version.

You'll need:

- 1 teaspoon honey
- A dash of vinegar
- 3 tablespoons evaporated milk

Mix the ingredients together in a bowl and cover your hair from root to tip. Wind a warm towel around your head and wait for twenty minutes before rinsing thoroughly. The milk will cleanse your hair, while the honey nourishes, and the vinegar adds a gloss.

- **Rinse, Rinse, Rinse.** Rinse your hair under the shower until the water runs completely clear to be sure no shampoo or conditioner is left behind – it will just make your hair look dull and drab again.

- **Get Brushing.** Groom your hair once or twice a day to remove built-up dirt and dead skin cells. Always brush thoroughly before you wash your hair to allow the shampoo to move easily through it.

Glamour Girl Tip: There's no point in brushing your shiny hair with a dirty brush. Wash your brushes and combs regularly in a bowl of warm water with a dollop of shampoo and leave them to dry on a towel.

HOW TO AIR-KISS

Make sure you make a cool impression when you bump into friends. It's time to perfect the celebrity-style air-kiss.

Start by making sure that you look delighted to see your friend. Smile and widen your eyes and tell her how lovely she looks. Call your friend "Darling," "Honey," and "Sweetheart." Finally, swoop toward her and almost touch her left cheek with yours and then her right cheek. Be sure to say "Mwah" loudly each time.

HOW TO MAKE YOUR OWN BUBBLE BATH

Bubbles make a bath a special treat and you can save money by making your own.

Mix together ½ cup of baby shampoo, ¾ cup of water, and a few pinches of salt. Stir in a few drops of essential oil (lavender, lemon, or peppermint are especially nice).

Pour the mixture into a pretty bottle. Use a plastic one that won't break if you drop it. Decorate the bottle with stickers and a pretty ribbon and enjoy your bath!

HOW TO TURN BATHTIME INTO A RELAXING TREAT

This bubble-icious bath is best taken just before bed. Get all your chores and homework done first so you can R-E-L-A-X.

SET THE SCENE

- Make sure the bathroom is warm and there is a clean towel ready.

- Have a cup of juice or water nearby so you can sip as you soak.

- Put on some soothing music. Classical music is very relaxing.

• Add a little scented bubble bath or oil to the running water, but be careful not to leave the bathtub slippery for the next person.

Glamour Girl Tip: The heads of flowers floating on the surface of the water add a serious touch of glamour.

R-E-L-A-X

Sink into the water and lie there for twenty minutes. Rest your head on a bath cushion or a rolled-up towel and breathe slowly and deeply. Lie there and imagine all the worries of your day dissolving into the water.

AFTERWARD

Pat your skin dry with a warm, soft towel. Smooth your skin with a little scented body lotion, taking special care of really dry areas like knees and elbows. Pull on your PJs and head straight for bed. Sprinkle a couple of drops of lavender oil on to your pillow to help you sleep peacefully.

HOW TO PERSUADE YOUR BEST FRIEND TO LEND YOU HER CLOTHES

A clever way to DOUBLE the size of your wardrobe is to share clothes with a friend. However, if your most stylish friend doesn't seem eager to let you borrow her clothes, here are some tips to help persuade her:

- Compliment her on her fantastic taste in clothes and tell her how much you'd love to be as well dressed as she is.

- Explain that you'd like to experiment with clothes more but you don't have enough money to buy lots of new things.

- Offer to let her take her pick of your wardrobe if she'll lend you something in return. (If you don't have many clothes, it may be best to wait until your friend has agreed to swap before you let her see the contents of your closet.)

- Promise to wash and iron her clothes before you give them back to her. Tell her you will even dry-clean them if necessary.

- Promise to give her clothes back on an agreed date – and stick to that date to ensure she's happy to swap with you again.

Glamour Girl Tip: Be very careful with your friend's clothes. If you ruin something, you'll have to replace it immediately or she'll never let you borrow anything again.

HOW TO QUICKLY SMOOTH AWAY DRY HANDS

Keep a tube of hand lotion by your bedside at all times and remember to apply a drop every morning and evening to keep your skin soft and smooth. But if your skin is still very dry, try this mini treat:

1. Fill the bathtub with warm water.

2. Cover your hands in oil – olive oil from the kitchen is fine, although manicurists prefer almond oil. Take the time to rub the oil into your nails, too, as it will help them to grow stronger.

3. Smooth on lots of rich hand lotion – it'll create a barrier around the oil and encourage it to sink into your skin.

4. Now soak in the bathtub for ten minutes, allowing your hands to rest in the water.

5. When you get out of the bathtub, gently rub your hands dry, then apply a few more drops of hand lotion.

You'll be amazed at the results!

HOW TO APPLY EYE SHADOW

When you're ready to start experimenting with makeup, it's a good idea to practice your technique at home before you unleash your new look on the world. Look for flattering, natural shades in a powder to highlight the color of your eyes:

Blue eyes: pastel pink or peach

Brown eyes: olive green or golden brown

Green eyes: lilac or gold

Hazel eyes: gray and mauve

First, make sure it's okay with your parents before you start wearing makeup. Most eyeshadows come in sets of two or three shades, which makes it even easier to find great colors to suit you.

Start with a little of the palest shade to highlight your brow line. Next brush the medium shade across your eyelid, avoiding the inner corner. Then use the darkest color around the crease to define the shape of your eye. Blend the colors where they meet.

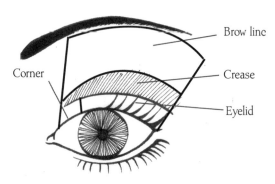

HOW TO DEAL WITH ZITS

Even supermodels sometimes get pimples. However, with a little know-how you can help a pimple heal quickly and make it almost invisible to the naked eye.

HOW TO CURE A PIMPLE

First, you should NEVER squeeze a pimple – it'll just look even more red and inflamed. What's more, you'll risk pushing the infection deeper into your skin and it may leave a permanent scar.

1. Wash your skin thoroughly and pat it dry with a clean towel.

2. Wrap an ice cube in a clean washcloth or towel and hold it over the spot for a minute or two; it'll help bring down the swelling.

3. Dip the end of a cotton swab into some diluted tea tree oil (available at any pharmacy) and dot a tiny amount directly onto the pimple.

4. Leave it alone to heal.

Glamour Girl Tip: If you keep getting pimples in the same area, it could be because that area is constantly in contact with a telephone, bicycle helmet, or sunglasses, which aren't spotlessly clean. Also, avoid touching your face with your hands repeatedly, as that can cause pimples to form.

HOW TO USE CONCEALER

Concealers are a great way to cover pimples and blemishes so your skin looks perfect. You can buy them from the makeup counter at most pharmacies and department stores. Don't choose one that's darker or lighter than your natural skin tone, or you'll draw more attention to the problem.

1. If the pimple is dry and crusty, apply a little petroleum jelly first to soften it.

2. Apply the concealer to the pimple using a clean cotton swab. (Don't apply concealer on areas around the spot that don't need it or you'll just create a "halo effect.")

3. Pat some face powder over the concealer to set it and help it stay put all day long.

Glamour Girl Tip: Don't apply concealer with your fingers or you'll risk spreading the infection.

IMPORTANT INFORMATION

If you feel you might be suffering from acne rather than just the occasional pimple, make an appointment with your family doctor or a dermatologist to ask for advice.

HOW TO MAKE YOUR OWN BODY GLITTER

This fabulous gel can be smoothed onto your body to make your skin shimmer. You can even smooth it through your hair for a gorgeous nighttime glow.

What you'll need:

• 1 teaspoon petroleum jelly

• 4 teaspoons aloe vera gel (available at pharmacies and health food stores)

- Ultrafine cosmetic-grade glitter (available at arts and crafts stores)
- A small jar. Baby food jars or spice bottles are ideal. Make sure they are thoroughly washed out in soapy water and then dried.
- A small bowl
- A spoon

How to make it:

1. Spoon the aloe vera gel into the bowl. Add the petroleum jelly to make it a little thicker. Stir well.

2. Sprinkle a few pinches of glitter into your mixture. Be sure the glitter is "cosmetic-grade," which means it's safe to use on your skin. Stir well.

3. Smooth a little onto the back of your hand to see if you like the effect.

4. If it's too glittery, add a little more aloe vera gel. If it's not glittery enough, add an extra pinch of glitter.

5. Spoon the mixture into your jar.

6. Smooth on the glitter whenever you like and glow, glow, glow!

HOW TO HAIL A TAXICAB

If you and your family take a trip to the city, you may need to hail a cab to get home. Follow these tips and you'll impress everyone with your incredible cab-hailing skills.

1. Make sure that someone in the family has plenty of cash to pay for the journey.

2. Stand out. Wearing bright colors will help. Stand confidently near the edge of the pavement in a spot where you and your family are easy to see from the street.

3. Keep an eye on the street for the next available taxi. Usually there will be a light on top of the car showing that the cab is not taken by another passenger.

4. As soon as you spot a cab, raise your arm and wave elegantly to catch the driver's attention. Never step into the street. Wait for the taxi to pull over to you.

5. Get into the cab and tell the driver your destination.

6. Sit back and relax. Your parents are impressed and you're on your way home.

Glamour Girl Tip: Make sure you only take a taxi when you are with your family and friends. It is safer that way, and you have a ready-made audience to wow.

HOW TO MAKE YOUR CLOTHES SMELL NICE

- Air out your clothes at the end of each day by putting them on a clothes hanger or on the back of a chair near an open window. Place your shoes on the windowsill at the same time, which will help prevent any unpleasant smells from developing.

- Place scented dryer sheets in your shoes when you're not wearing them to keep them smelling fresh.

- Unwrap a bar of scented soap and place it in the bottom of your closet as an instant clothes freshener.

- Add a few drops of perfume to the final rinse of your wash. Your clothes, sheets, and towels will all smell sweet and fragrant.

Glamour Girl Tip: Never, ever mix up clean clothes and dirty ones. Put dirty clothes into a laundry bag or basket right away so they are ready to be washed.

HOW TO JAZZ UP A BORING PONYTAIL

A simple ponytail can be turned into lots of new styles. With a little know-how and some practice, you'll soon have the best ponytail around.

WRAP IT

Pull a strand of hair out of your ponytail. Wrap it around the top of your ponytail until the hair elastic is hidden. Secure it in place with a hair clip.

KNOT IT

Separate your ponytail into six to eight sections. Twist each section around and around until it forms a loose knot. Pin each knot randomly onto the back of your head.

CURL IT

Curl the ends of your ponytail with velcro rollers. Simply twist the rollers into slightly damp hair and leave them in until it's dry. When you remove the rollers, spritz the curls with hair spray to help them last all day.

CRIMP IT

Pull a few random strands of hair loose from your ponytail. Ask an adult for help crimping them with a heated crimping iron. Then let the tendrils fall loosely around your face.

BRAID IT

Simply braid a ponytail and secure the end with a hair elastic or pretty hair clip.

ACCESSORIZE IT

Grab some pretty clips, hair ornaments, or other hair jewels and attach them all around the base of your ponytail. Alternatively, brush your hair into a low-slung ponytail at the nape of your neck. Tuck a few feathers (peacock feathers are fantastic) into the hair elastic.

DIP IT

Use temporary hair dye (the sort that washes out right away — not permanent or semipermanent). Follow the instructions on the package carefully, but only apply the dye to the ends of your hair. It should look as though your ponytail has been dipped in color. Experiment with funky colors like black, red, or orange!

HOW TO HAVE A GOOD NIGHT'S SLEEP

A good night's sleep helps you feel great and look gorgeous. Most glamorous girls need around ten hours of sleep each night. Try this mini bedtime routine to help you fall asleep easily.

HAVE A LIGHT SNACK

Sweet treats, heavy meals, and sugary drinks just before bed will keep you awake. If your tummy's rumbling, have some warm milk, a banana, or a slice of whole wheat toast an hour before bed. A cup of peppermint or chamomile tea will help you relax, too.

WIND DOWN

Try to relax during the hour before bed by reading a book or listening to some gentle music. Make sure you get your homework done earlier in the evening – doing it just before bed will leave your mind racing and keep you awake.

MAKE SURE YOUR BEDROOM'S DARK AND QUIET

Make sure the curtains are pulled tight and get rid of any ticking clocks. If you live in a noisy household, make a DO NOT DISTURB sign for your bedroom door and use it.

PREPARE FOR BED

Put a glass of water by your bed in case you wake up thirsty. Pull on some comfy PJs, wash your face, brush your teeth, and hop between the sheets. Read for a while until you feel nice and sleepy, then turn out the light.

GET COMFORTABLE

Make sure your neck is well supported with one or two soft pillows. Don't wrap yourself up in too many blankets – you don't want to get too hot during the night.

LET YOUR WORRIES FLOAT AWAY

Worrying can keep you awake. If you're anxious about something, try this trick: Imagine you're putting the problem into a box. Then imagine you're putting the box into a closet and locking it away until morning. This will often help you relax enough to fall asleep.

Sleep tight!

HOW TO BATHE LIKE CLEOPATRA

Cleopatra, the queen of ancient Egypt, was said to bathe in milk. You, too, can take a milk bath to soothe and soften your skin.

Just add 2 pints of whole milk (about 4 cups) to a tub of warm water. Swirl it around thoroughly so that the water becomes white. Hop in and have a good soak for at least twenty minutes. Rinse in clear, cool water.

HOW TO DO A PERFECT PIROUETTE

Find a good place to practice your pirouette. Carpets are not ideal, so try the tiled floor in your kitchen or bathroom. Make sure there's enough space so that if you fall, you won't crash into something and hurt yourself.

Start with your left foot turned out and the heel of your right foot against the toes. This is called fifth position.

Lift your right arm as though you are hugging a beach ball to your chest and hold your left arm out to the side, slightly curved toward your body.

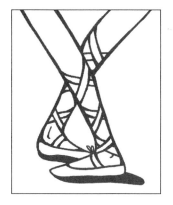

Now keep your back straight, and in one movement, bend your knees outward in a *plié*, pushing up onto the tiptoes of your left foot and bringing your right foot up to your knee with your toes pointed. At the same time, use your momentum to spin clockwise.

When you have turned in a full circle, lower yourself off your tiptoes and onto your left foot. Then bring your right leg back into its original fifth position. Always make sure the weight of your body is on your supporting leg when you finish your pirouette.

Glamour Girl Tip: It's a good idea to learn how to spot so that you don't get dizzy spinning around. Practice slowly at first to get the technique just right. Keep your eyes on one spot on the wall in front of you. Slowly spin your body around, keeping your head in the same position until you can't turn anymore. Then whip your head around at the last possible second to the same spot again while you continue to turn.

35

HOW TO MAKE
SOAP-ON-A-ROPE

Hanging the soap up in the shower means it's always easy to find. Soap-on-a-rope makes a great gift, too.

You'll need:

- Three bars of white soap
- Cheese grater
- Bowl and jug
- Piece of rope or ribbon
- Waxed or parchment paper
- Rubber gloves
- Food coloring (optional)

1. Finely grate the soap into a large bowl.

2. Fill the jug with warm water. If you want to make colored soap, add a few drops of your chosen food coloring to the water. Don't overdo it though, or you'll find your skin changing color as you wash!

3. Slowly add drops of the warm water to the soap flakes until it's the consistency of thick oatmeal.

4. Pull on the rubber gloves and mix well with your hands.

5. Cut the rope or ribbon to your chosen length (10–12 inches is ideal) and lay on the waxed paper.

6. Pat the soap mixture around one end of the rope in a ball shape, making sure the rope is in the center of the soap ball.

7. Once you're happy with the shape, leave the soap to dry for around twenty-four hours.

8. Tie a loop in the other end of the rope so that you can hang it up in the shower.

Glamour Girl Tip: You can add a handful of other ingredients to the soap mixture if you like:

• Dried flowers look and smell very pretty.

• Oats turn a simple soap into an effective body scrub.

• Grated lemon peel makes a refreshing soap that will really wake you up in the morning.

HOW TO GET THE FLUTTERIEST LASHES

A coat of mascara is the best way to create a fluttering fringe to your eyes, especially if you have light-colored hair and your lashes are hard to notice.

Most mascaras are applied with a spiral brush at the end of a wand. This makes them quick and easy to use. Some contain fibers to add extra thickness and length to your lashes. For a girl on the go, waterproof mascara is the best choice. It will withstand tears, showers, and swimming, but you'll need a special makeup remover to take it off.

1. Start by applying mascara to your upper lashes. Brush them downward to begin with, then brush the lashes upward from underneath. Use a tiny zigzag movement from side to side to prevent the mascara from clumping.

2. With the tip of the mascara wand, brush your lower lashes, using a gentle side-to-side technique. You can keep your hand steady by resting your elbow on a firm surface. If you've got a shaky hand, try holding the edge of a tissue under your eyelashes while

applying mascara to prevent it from smudging onto your skin.

3. Comb through your lashes with an eyelash comb to remove any small lumps of mascara. This will prevent your lashes from clumping together.

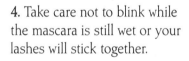

4. Take care not to blink while the mascara is still wet or your lashes will stick together.

5. Repeat the whole process once or twice more to create a really fluttery effect.

39

HOW TO FIGURE OUT YOUR FACE SHAPE

Different hairstyles suit different face shapes. The four main face shapes are oval, round, heart-shaped, and square.

To figure out what shape your face is, pull all your hair back with a headband. Look in a mirror and trace around the outline of your face with a lipstick (the sharp edge of a bar of soap will work well, too). Move away from the mirror and look carefully at the shape. Decide which shape your face is most similar to, then check out the descriptions below and choose your ideal hairstyles. (Don't forget to clean the mirror afterward!)

OVAL

Any style suits an oval face, so you
can try really dramatic looks like
ultrashort bobs as well as long,
straight hair.

ROUND

HEART-SHAPED

Chin-length bobs, soft layers,
and side parts work well
with round faces.

SQUARE

Try neat styles with flipped-
up ends. Long wispy bangs,
waves, or short and spiky
cuts would also work well
for you.

Go for soft layers, curls, or
side-swept parts.

HOW TO MAKE YOUR EYES LOOK BRIGHTER

If you're feeling tired and you've stared at a computer screen for too long or you're simply fighting off a cold, your eyes might start to look really red. Here's a simple three-step plan to make them sparkle again:

1. A lack of water can make your eyes look really tired, so drink six to eight glasses of water every day to keep the redness away.

2. Empty an ice cube tray into a sink of cold water and soak a towel in it. Wring the cold towel out, then lie down and place it over your eyes for five minutes. If the towel gets too warm, soak it in the ice water again and repeat.

3. Apply a dot of pale, pearly eyeshadow on the skin at the inner corner of your eye and just above your pupil. This will make your eyes look wider and brighter even if you're still sleepy.

HOW TO PLAN A THEME PARTY

When it's time to celebrate, it can be a great idea for you and your friends to throw a themed party. Get permission from the adults first and then start planning!

- Choosing your theme might depend on the season, such as Halloween, Christmas, or Summer Fun. Or you can just make one up. Good ideas include Think Pink, Superheroes, Hawaiian, or Hollywood themes. You can even base a party theme on your favorite TV show or on a particular era in history (ancient Roman, ancient Egyptian, or the seventies, for example).

- Send out your invitations well in advance and include all the information your guests need to know about the party and theme. Ask people to RSVP (this is French for *Répondez S'il Vous Plaît*, which means they need to reply). Then you'll know how many guests to expect.

- The party decorations should go with your theme. For instance, carve pumpkins for Halloween, hang pink balloons and ribbons for a Think Pink party, and hang a disco ball and a tie-dyed tapestry for a seventies party.

- Keep your guests entertained with plenty of party games and dancing.

- It's a good idea to have music ready to keep the atmosphere lively. If you don't have lots of your own CDs, you could ask your guests to bring along their favorites to dance to.

HOW TO MAKE A BAG CHARM

Glam up a plain handbag or a boring old backpack with a safety pin charm. It couldn't be easier.

What you'll need:

- 30 safety pins in various sizes
- Beads of various sizes
- Piece of thin elastic about 6 inches long

GET BEADING

1. Open up a safety pin. Thread as many beads as you can onto the pin. Get creative with the pattern!

2. Close the pin carefully.

3. Repeat this process for as many safety pins as you have.

4. Knot a bead on one end of the piece of elastic.

5. Now start threading the beaded safety pins onto the elastic. Thread some through the top end of the pin, some through the bottom end, and some through the middle.

6. Finish off with two beads, secured with a knot.

7. Tie the remaining end of the elastic thread onto your bag.

HOW TO GIVE YOURSELF A MINI FACIAL

Every couple of weeks, set aside a bit of time to give yourself a relaxing salon-style facial at home. It'll help keep skin deep-down clean and super soft.

1. Smooth your skin with cleansing cream, gentle soap, or facial wash. Leave it on for one or two minutes to give it time to dissolve grime and makeup, then wipe away with a clean, damp towel.

2. Massage a blob of facial scrub or some dry, uncooked oatmeal over your skin to whisk away dead surface skin cells and clear blocked pores. Rinse away with warm water.

3. Fill a bowl with freshly boiled water (ask an adult to supervise this part). Then lean over the bowl, capturing the steam by placing a towel over your head. Stay there for five minutes to allow the steam to warm and soften your skin. Those with sensitive skin should skip this step.

4. Splash your face with warm water and pat dry.

5. Smooth on a homemade fruit facial:

   If you have oily skin: Crush six strawberries with a fork, smooth onto your face, and leave on for three minutes.

If you have normal/dry skin: Crush a peeled banana with a fork, smooth onto your face, and leave on for five minutes.

6. Remove the mask with a clean tissue, then rinse your face with warm water.

7. Finish with a splash of cool water to freshen your skin. Pat dry with a towel.

8. Dot your skin with moisturizer and massage it in to encourage a brighter complexion.

HOW TO TELL A FRIEND SHE'S MADE A FASHION ERROR

Too shy to tell a friend her top is on inside out or her shirt is buttoned up wrong? Don't be – she'll be less embarrassed if a good friend tells her right away rather than letting her walk around looking really silly all day long. And you never know when you might need her to do the same favor for you!

Plan ahead. Get together with your friends and make up some subtle hand signals to warn one another – you could tug on your earlobe or sing a snippet from your favorite song. That way you'll know that you have one another's backs just in case the worst happens.

If you haven't prepared in advance for a fatal fashion disaster, then the best thing to do is to quickly grab your friend and point out the error quietly.

HANDY HINTS

• Compliment your friend on how well she handled the situation.

• Point out how great her taste in clothes is, so who cares if someone laughed?

• Change the subject as soon as you can.

Glamour Girl Tip: Don't actually point. This will only draw attention to the situation and embarrass your friend even more.

THINGS TO AVOID

• Any kind of laughter – this will only draw attention to the problem.

• Telling other people first – this is a quick way to end a friendship.

• Doing an impression of how embarrassed your friend was.

HOW TO CUSTOMIZE A T-SHIRT WITH FABRIC PAINTS

Wear your art on your sleeve as well as on the rest of your T-shirt by getting crafty with some fabric pens. They allow you to paint directly onto the fabric without any mixing or mess, and you can get them from most arts and crafts stores.

Here's how:

1. You'll need a plain T-shirt. Choose a plain white or pastel-colored one so that your design shows up really well.

2. Practice your design on a piece of paper first. You could try graffiti-style, designing your own logo, or just drawing a simple, bold image like a face or a sun.

3. Now you're ready to paint your T-shirt. Put a piece of thick paper or cardboard inside the T-shirt so that the ink doesn't leak through from the front to the back.

4. Draw your image on the T-shirt.

5. When you use fabric pens, you need to iron your finished design to help set it. Check with an adult for advice or help before you do this.

Glamour Girl Tip: Once you've invested in a set of fabric pens, you can make use of them on lots of projects. Why not decorate your jeans or pillowcases? (Just be sure to get an adult's permission first!)

HOW TO CONVINCE PEOPLE YOU'RE A CELEBRITY

- Wear huge sunglasses that practically cover your whole face, even when you're inside the house.

- Go to school with a film crew (your kid brother and his friends will do). Explain to your teacher that you're the subject of a brand-new reality TV show.

- Carry a huge handbag with a dog the size of a hamster in it. (A stuffed dog will do.)

- Apply fake tan from head to toe until you are bright orange.

- Wear very silly shoes.

- Be unreasonable wherever you go. You could tell the lunch ladies you're on a special diet and can only eat blue food, or tell your teacher you didn't finish your homework because you were practicing your Oscar acceptance speech.

- Get your parents to tint the windows of the family car.

- Travel with an entourage (a group of friends) at all times to help you with any boring tasks.

HOW TO TURN AN OLD PAIR OF JEANS INTO A FAB SKIRT

Here's the perfect way to recycle an old pair of jeans you don't like anymore into a skirt you'll love:

1. Take the pair of jeans and cut straight across both legs at the length you would like your skirt to be.

2. Cut carefully up the inside seam of each leg and trim off the extra fabric. At the front, cut to just below the fly and overlap the curved sections. At the back, cut to about 2 inches below the waistband.

3. On a flat surface, overlap the curved sections at the front and back and sew into place.

4. From one of the pieces of cast-off legs, cut a triangle large enough to fill the gap between the legs (alternatively, you could use a pretty cotton fabric to contrast with the denim).

5. Either sew the triangles to the insides of the legs by hand or use a sewing machine.

6. Don't bother hemming the bottom of the skirt if you want to wear it right away – the frayed look is very cool.

Glamour Girl Tip: If you're feeling creative, sew a length of ribbon or lace trim around the hem to add an extra touch of glamour.

HOW TO PERSUADE YOUR PARENTS TO LET YOU HAVE YOUR EARS PIERCED

If you really want to get your ears pierced, you need to get permission first. It's worth planning in advance how to get your parents on your side. Whatever you do, don't let a friend pierce your ears for you – it's unhygienic and you might get an infection.

• Before you start on your campaign to convince your parents, be sure you really do want your ears pierced. There are some great clip-on earrings available that look just as good.

- Do your research first. The more knowledge you have, the easier it'll be to persuade your parents.

- Offer to pay for it yourself or suggest it would be a great birthday present.

- Visit a couple of ear-piercing shops with your parents first. They will be able to see who would do the procedure and the equipment that's used. Let your parents choose which place they prefer.

- Don't burst into tears or throw a tantrum if they refuse. Leave it for a while and ask again. Perhaps you'll eventually be able to persuade them to set a date when they'll allow you to have your ears pierced.

HOW TO TAKE CARE OF NEWLY PIERCED EARS

Pierced ears might look good, but infected ears do not. Here's how to look after your newly-pierced lobes properly:

- Make sure your first pair of earrings has gold or surgical steel posts (that's the part of the earring that goes through the hole). Gold posts or surgical steel are less likely to cause infection and swelling.

- When you first get your ears pierced, you should leave the earrings in for six weeks until your ears are completely healed. If you don't, your holes could close up and you'll have to go through everything all over again!

- Don't fiddle with your earrings during the healing process.

- Apply antiseptic lotion to your ears in the morning and at night – you should be given some by the person who pierced your ears. Wash your hands first, then apply the lotion to your ears with a clean cotton swab.

- Finally, rotate each earring once every morning and night.

WHAT IF YOUR EARS GET INFECTED?

An infected earlobe may be swollen, red, warm, and painful or oozing fluid. If you think one of your pierced ears may be infected, tell an adult immediately. He or she will probably want to check with your family doctor for advice on how to deal with the infection. Follow any advice carefully to ensure the infection heals completely.

HOW TO SHAMPOO AND CONDITION YOUR HAIR PROPERLY

Scientists have worked out exactly how you should wash and condition your hair. After experimenting on hundreds of people, they came up with the following instructions:

SHAMPOOING

- Dampen your hair with running water warmed to a temperature of precisely 98°F.

- Use exactly the right amount of shampoo: 1 teaspoon of shampoo for short hair, 1½ teaspoons for medium-length hair, and 2 teaspoons for long hair.

- Lather hair for 27 seconds, rubbing it twenty times with your fingertips.

- Rinse your hair for twenty-two seconds in water that's 98°F.

- Repeat the whole process.

CONDITIONING

- Use ½ teaspoon of conditioner for short hair, ¾ teaspoon for medium-length hair, and 1 teaspoon for long hair.

- Apply conditioner with a wide-toothed comb.

- Let the conditioner sink in for fifty-seven seconds before rinsing with water at 98°F.

- Pat your hair dry with a towel to absorb excess water before leaving it to dry naturally.

HOW TO GET SUPER-SOFT FEET WHILE YOU SLEEP

DID YOU KNOW?

- There are twenty-six bones in each of your feet.

- Each time your feet touch the floor, double the weight of your body impacts with the floor.

- More than 50 percent of people don't like their feet, often as a result of foot problems.

- Your feet contain around 250,000 sweat glands and they perspire more than any other part of your body. Each foot produces an egg-cup-full of sweat each day.

- In your lifetime, it's estimated that your feet will carry you 68,000 miles or almost three times around the world.

Indulge your feet with the following treat once a week and they'll always be soft and smooth.

1. Rub your feet with a layer of rich foot lotion. If you prefer, you can make your own by mixing ¼ cup olive oil, ¼ cup light cream and 1 tablespoon mayonnaise.

2. Pull on a pair of socks and head for bed.

3. Wash off the cream in the morning to reveal beautifully soft tootsies.

4. Don't forget to put the socks in the wash!

HOW TO GROW YOUR NAILS SUCCESSFULLY

Nibbling your nails can be a hard habit to break, but it's well worth trying if you'd like to grow elegantly long and strong nails. Here are some tips to help you:

• Restrict yourself to biting the nails on just one hand and then on only one nail. You'll soon be inspired to grow out the bitten one.

• Regularly apply scented hand lotion or an anti-nail-biting cream. The unpleasant flavor will keep you from gnawing your nails.

• If your parents and school allow it, try using stick-on nails for a few weeks so your nails have a chance to grow underneath.

HEALTHY NAILS

Once you've broken a nail-biting habit, follow these pointers to keep your nails strong and beautiful:

• Eat two portions of protein a day. Meat, fish, dairy, soy, and beans will all help your nails to grow strong and healthy.

• When you wash the dishes, always wear latex gloves, as soaking your hands in water weakens the nails.

• When your nails begin to grow, keep them in shape with a nail file or an emery board to keep them from breaking.

• Make sure your nails are dry, then gently smooth away any rough edges and file them into a nice, even shape.

• Never file down into the sides of your nails, as it can lead to infection and seriously weaken your nails.

• Don't use your nails as a tool. Find the right tool for the job rather than risk having to grow your nail from scratch again.

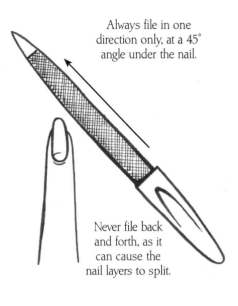

Always file in one direction only, at a 45° angle under the nail.

Never file back and forth, as it can cause the nail layers to split.

• Once a week, soak your bare nails in a bowl of olive oil for ten minutes. Then wipe away the excess oil with a cotton ball.

DID YOU KNOW?

• Nails grow about ⅛ inch a month.

• Nails grow faster in summer than in winter.

• If you've lost a nail due to an accident, it'll take about six months to grow back.

• Your middle fingernail grows the quickest while your thumbnail grows the slowest.

• A child's nails grow more quickly than an adult's.

• Toenails grow more slowly than fingernails.

HOW TO CONVINCE PEOPLE YOU'RE A HAND MODEL

Just having beautiful hands isn't enough to convince people you're a hand model – you have to act the part as well. Follow these tips to convince your friends that your hands are your fortune. You'll also have a ready-made excuse for avoiding all sorts of boring tasks.

• Refuse to do anything that might damage your hands. This can include doing the dishes (dries out the skin), writing essays (you could get ink on your fingers), and taking the dog for a walk (the dog's leash could cause calluses to form on your hands).

• Gather together a handful of props like a lipstick, a cup of coffee, and a box of laundry detergent. Get your best friend to take close-up pictures of your hands holding the props, just like in magazine ads. Mount the results in a photograph album and, *voilà*: your very own portfolio.

- Wear white cotton manicure gloves to protect your hands at all times.

- Practice hand-modeling poses whenever anyone's around. Don't just pass your mom a magazine she wants to read – strike a "hand pose" as you do it.

- Take up music lessons. Playing a musical instrument helps to encourage steady hands, which are vital for photographic shoots that can go on for hours.

- Insist that you have Jell-O after every meal. Hand models say the gelatin in it is good for strengthening nails.

- Change the color of your nail polish each night. After all, you need a new look for every single photo shoot.

- Get your parents to insure your hands for a million dollars.

HOW TO SHAPE YOUR NAILS TO SUIT YOUR HANDS

When you're filing your nails, make sure you consider your overall hand shape and pick a file style that suits you best.

- If you have small hands, go for almond-shaped nails.

- If you have short, wide fingers, aim for an oval shape with a squared-off tip.

- If you have large hands or wide nails, try squared-off ends.

HOW TO BE THE BEST BRIDESMAID

It's a real honor to be asked to be someone's bridesmaid or flower girl. Here's how to impress the bride on her big day.

Smile sweetly when you see your dress for the first time. It doesn't matter if you hate lime green satin – it's the bride's choice. Just comment on how stylish of her it was to match your dress to her bouquet.

Have something to eat and drink before you put on your outfit. That way you won't spoil it with crumbs and you'll have energy to get through the day. It might be a long time before you get a chance to eat again.

Offer to look after younger bridesmaids or flower girls if there are any. Very young children have a habit of playing hide-and-seek under the bride's dress and bursting into tears during the ceremony.

If the bride has a long skirt and veil, make sure it's all straight before she walks down the aisle. If you're the maid of honor, you'll need to take the bride's bouquet during the ceremony, then hand it back to her afterward.

Offer to help out with small chores during the day, such as getting the bride a drink of water while she's getting ready or handing out favors to guests later on.

Most of all, smile and enjoy yourself.

HOW TO WALK WITH CONFIDENCE

The best way to make people think you're brimming with self-assurance and poise is to strut like a star. Follow these steps to get the best out of your stride:

1. Imagine that someone is pulling your head up with a long piece of string, push your shoulders back, and smile.

2. Think of a fast-paced, lively song that you love and sing the tune in your head, or out loud if you prefer.

3. Gently start swinging your arms and walk along to the rhythm of your song, bouncing a little at the knees.

4. Remember to smile and wave when heads turn to look your way.

HOW TO CRY AT A WEDDING

There's nothing like a happy occasion to bring out smiles and tears. Here's how to get your fill of crying without upstaging the bride:

- Take a pretty cotton hanky with you rather than an old tissue. Use it to dab gently at your eyes if you start to well up.

- Remember to smile and breathe while you are crying. You don't want to make a scary face at a wedding!

- It's important not to sob too loudly or blow your nose noisily. This may prevent everyone else from enjoying the ceremony.

- Don't cry for too long or people will start to worry about you rather than thinking about how beautiful the bride is.

HOW TO GET RID OF PUFFY EYES

If you've got a cold, hay fever, or you're just really tired, try this de-puffing trick.

Place a clean teaspoon in a glass of ice water. After a few minutes, remove it and hold the spoon against your closed eyes until they feel cooler and brighter.

HOW TO PRETEND YOU HAVE FRECKLES

If you have freckles, never try to hide them. Freckles make you look naturally pretty and sun-kissed. If you're not lucky enough to have freckles, there's an easy way to fake them.

1. Start by making sure that your skin is really clean.

2. Choose a light brown eyebrow pencil if you have pale skin or a deeper shade if you have darker skin.

3. Sharpen the eyebrow pencil and dot a few freckles onto your face, concentrating them around your nose and cheeks.

4. To make your fake freckles look more realistic, apply different sized dots and soften the edges with a clean cotton swab.

5. Dust your skin with a little face powder to set the fake freckles in place.

Glamour Girl Tip: For a speedy way to create an impression, just draw on a beauty mark. Take a black eyebrow pencil and apply a firm dot to your skin about ¾ inch from your top lip, then set it with a little face powder.

HOW TO EXIT A LIMO GRACEFULLY

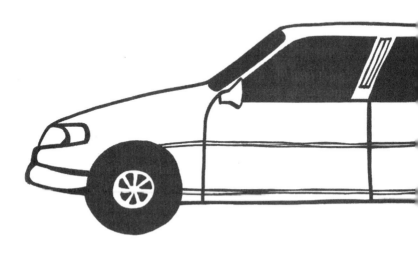

Once you're a celebrity, you'll be invited everywhere, and a stretch limousine is definitely the best way to arrive. But when all your fans and photographers are waiting to see you, it's important to learn how to get out of the car gracefully.

1. Open the door on the sidewalk side and check to be sure there's room for you to get out easily. Don't let camera flashes distract you.

2. While staying seated, swing both feet out onto the pavement. Use the door handle and the frame of the car to gently push yourself up in one smooth movement. Do not rush this step.

3. Remember to tilt your head forward a little to avoid banging it on the door frame as you stand up straight.

4. Shake out your dress to make sure you haven't wrinkled it, then turn toward your waiting fans to smile, wave, and head for the red carpet zone.

5. Pause for a moment or two for the waiting photographers and film crews. Don't forget to strike a pose (see page 117).

6. Remember to stop and give a few quick autographs to some of your fans before heading in to your glamorous event.

HOW TO MAKE A RIBBON BELT

Jazz up your old jeans with a pretty braided belt made from strands of colorful ribbon. Here's how to do it:

1. Look for ribbon that's about 1-inch wide.

2. Choose three different colors that look good together.

3. Measure around your waist. That's the length you should cut each ribbon piece. Cut three pieces in each color to this length.

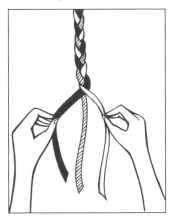

4. Take a strand of each color. Tie them together in a knot at one end. Lay them on a table and start braiding. You can braid it loosely or tightly – it's up to you!

5. Tie a knot at the end of the braid.

6. Repeat steps 4 and 5 to form two more braids from the remaining ribbon pieces.

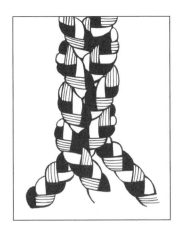

7. Now braid the three braids together to make a fat ribbon belt. Secure each end with a knot.

8. Simply thread the belt through the loops of your jeans and show off your new style. Tie the two ends together to secure.

Glamour Girl Tip: To create a more glamorous effect, just cut the ribbon strands a little longer and leave the ends loose to flutter around. You can even add a selection of pretty, glittery beads for some extra sparkle.

HOW TO CLEAN YOUR MAKEUP BRUSHES

Makeup brushes are the best way to apply makeup, and they should be cleaned regularly. Wash them every week or two to keep your brushes clean and your face healthy.

1. Squirt a little shampoo into a cup and fill it with warm water.

2. Swish the brushes in the water to dissolve any dirt and grime.

3. Rinse the brushes under a running tap until the water runs clear.

4. Gently squeeze the brushes with your fingers to remove excess moisture.

5. Place a clean towel on a flat surface and lay the brushes on top.

6. Leave them to air-dry.

HOW TO MAKE YOUR BEDROOM SKIN-FRIENDLY

Central heating can draw the moisture out of your skin, leaving it dry and dull, but there's a simple way to prevent this.

Keep the air moist in your bedroom by placing a well-watered houseplant on your windowsill or by keeping a bowl of water near a radiator. This way the water will gradually evaporate and humidify the air, keeping your skin moist.

HOW TO GET THE HAIR YOU REALLY WANT

If you're growing out your hair, it can be difficult to avoid a few bad-hair days until you get the style you want. Have a regular trim to snip away split ends and keep your hair looking healthy. Tell your stylist what look you're aiming for. He or she will be able to trim your hair to help you reach your goal as quickly as possible.

It's easy to end up with a haircut you don't like unless you tell your stylist exactly what you want. Follow these tips to avoid a really terrible hair day:

• Don't be shy about showing the stylist a photograph of the hairstyle you'd like. Be prepared for him or her to explain that the style might not suit your hair type or face shape, and try to find a good compromise.

• Always use your fingers to show the stylist how long you want your hair, how much you want cut off, and the shape you prefer.

- Don't bury your nose in a magazine while your hair is being cut. Watch what your stylist is doing and politely but firmly stop your stylist if he or she is about to do something you know you won't like.

- Take a good look in the mirror when your stylist has finished. It's your last chance to point out any problems and give your stylist the opportunity to fix things.

Remember: a good diet, regular exercise, and plenty of sleep will encourage your hair to grow more quickly. Experiment with different looks as your hair goes through different lengths, and invest in hair clips and headbands to add extra style as it grows.

HOW TO GROW OUT YOUR BANGS

- Start wearing your bangs away from your face right away. Use clips or a headband to keep loose strands out of your eyes.

- Part your hair to the side so that your bangs still look stylish as they grow out.

- Consider having some face-framing layers cut into the rest of your hair to help balance out your bangs as they grow.

HOW TO CREATE YOUR OWN PERSONAL STYLE

Following fashion slavishly can cost a small fortune. Be creative and thrifty and come up with a fabulous style of your very own.

- Look for inspiration in magazines and on TV, then select the things you like most.

- Pick and choose the things you like and imagine how you can combine them into a style of your own.

- Lay all your clothes out in your room and sort them into piles of things that suit you and things you'd like to adapt.

- Try changing the length or adding extra trim to items that are old and dull.

- Experiment with unusual combinations and try layering or adding accessories.

- Scope out thrift stores for inexpensive items that suit your style. This is a great way to find cool vintage clothes. It's also the greenest way to shop because you'll be recycling.

HOW TO ACCESSORIZE FABULOUSLY

You'll be surprised how many accessories you already have lying around at home. Anything from scarves and belts to brooches and bracelets can be used to add instant pizzazz to your wardrobe. Most of these ideas can be achieved with items you already own, so you shouldn't need to spend any extra money.

• Tie the ends of a long scarf together and hook your left arm into the loop, then bring the scarf across your back and hook your right arm into the other end to make an instant shrug.

• If last year's coat is looking a bit bedraggled, jazz it up with a pretty brooch or a fabric flower. Pin it onto a lapel or somewhere just below your collar bone.

• If your hair is misbehaving, why not just cover it up? Take a scarf or a pretty top and wrap it around your head like a turban or a bandanna. For extra sparkle, pin on a glamorous brooch just above your forehead.

• When a cold winter breeze is getting to you, simply fold your scarf in half, loop it around your neck, and slip the ends through the loop for a superstylish (and warm) look.

• Gather together all of the bangles and bracelets you own and put them all on at once. They'll be very eye-catching and they'll make a great clinking noise at the same time.

• A pretty silk or chiffon scarf can be used for lots of different things. Knot it at the neck, tie it at the waist, or loop it around your wrist and tie it in a stylish bow.

HOW TO KEEP CHLORINE IN SWIMMING POOLS FROM DAMAGING YOUR HAIR

Swimming is a fantastic way to stay in shape, but it can wreak havoc on your hair. That's because the water in most swimming pools contains a chemical called chlorine that kills germs in the water and makes it safe to swim in. The trouble with chlorine, though, is that it can make your hair dull, dry, and unmanageable.

• Coat your hair with some conditioner, then pull on a swimming cap to protect it from the chlorine in the pool.

• If you're too vain to wear a swimming cap, make sure you wet your hair under the shower before you get into the water. That way your hair will already be soaked and, as a result, will absorb much less of the chlorinated water.

• As soon as you get out of the pool, wash your hair using a special swimmer's shampoo that contains ingredients to help remove the chlorine.

• Use loads of conditioner after swimming to guard against the drying effects of chlorine.

Glamour Girl Tip: Chlorine can actually make blonde hair look a little green. If you have blonde hair and find this happens to you, ask an adult to dissolve four soluble aspirin in a jug of water. Pour it over your hair and leave in for five minutes before rinsing. The juice of a lemon or a little vinegar in 2 cups of water works well, too.

HOW TO HAVE THE PRETTIEST SUMMER FEET

- Choose three pretty shades of polish that go well together (pastels work best).

- Apply one coat of the first shade all over your toenails. Allow it to dry.

- Grab the second shade and paint a dot of color in the center of each nail.

- Take the third color and place several dots around the center like the petals of a flower.

- Allow the polish to dry.

- Show off your new look by slipping on a pair of pretty flip-flops.

HOW TO HOST A SPA-STYLE PARTY

Impress and pamper your friends by inviting them over for a relaxing and luxurious spa night. Ask everyone to bring a robe, flip-flops, headbands, a mirror, and a washcloth.

Create the right mood by covering any chairs and tables with white sheets. Use lamps or, better still, strands of white holiday

lights to create a relaxing atmosphere. Switch on some calming music. Check out your local library for special CDs that are designed for relaxation (forest or ocean sounds are particularly mellow).

Prepare some healthy spa-style snacks and drinks. Sparkling water or fruit juices look good in pretty glasses with colorful straws. Make special ice cubes to add to the drinks the day before. Pop slices of strawberry, lemon, or lime into each section of an ice cube tray, then add water and freeze. A selection of fruit, popcorn, and little sandwiches are good choices for spa-style snacks.

Glamour Girl Tip: Snacks on toothpicks (like cheese cubes or berries) are a great idea – your guests will find them easier to pick up if they have wet nail polish.

SPA TREATMENTS

Gather together a group of parents or siblings to act as spa staff. Get them to set up separate beauty stations offering different treatments. Create a poster board to outline which treatments are available, and let your guests pick the three they would like.

Nifty Nails. File away rough edges from nails with an emery board. Slick on clear nail polish, then sprinkle on some glitter while the polish is still wet. Seal with a second coat of polish.

Sensational Stripes. Get a tube of hair mascara or some brightly colored eyelash mascara. Comb it through dry hair for instant, washable highlights. This looks great if you concentrate the color in the front sections of your guest's hair.

Magical Masks. For each mask, mix together a teaspoon of honey, 3 tablespoons of plain yogurt, and a few drops of lemon juice. Apply to clean skin and pop cucumber slices over the eyes. Relax for five minutes and then rinse.

Fruity Feet. Add a few drops of fruit-scented bubble bath to a large bowl of warm water. Have your guest soak her feet for five minutes. Pat her feet dry, then give her a foot massage using a few drops of olive oil or body lotion.

Glamorous Lashes. Start by curling your friend's eyelashes with a metal eyelash curler. Be gentle and be sure not to pinch her skin or pull on the lashes. Then slick on a coat of clear mascara to add extra definition.

Glamour Girl Tip: Before your guests leave, take a photo of each girl to show the quality of your spa. Pour everyone a cup of bedtime herbal tea so your guests are sure to enjoy a good night's sleep when they get home.

HOW TO CREATE YOUR OWN DRESSING TABLE

Create a little oasis of calm in your bedroom by organizing all of your beauty products. Any table, shelf, or windowsill will do. You can even set everything up on a tray covered with a piece of pretty fabric. Whatever you choose, the same rules apply:

• Too many things on display will look cluttered and gather dust. Keep your favorite items on show and store everything else in a selection of pretty boxes or bags – decorated plastic bins and pencil cases are ideal.

• A cutlery tray makes it easy for you to organize all your supplies into sections – hair clips in one section, nail polish in another, etc. You can store it in a drawer or slide it under your bed and just bring it out whenever you need it.

• Try to get a good-size mirror. It can be hand-held, freestanding, or attached to a wall. You'll never look your best if you're constantly peering into a tiny compact-size mirror.

• Make sure your dressing table is close to a good light source so that you can see what you're doing.

• Decorate your dressing table with a few pretty ornaments. Why not arrange shells from the seaside or a few wildflowers in a jar?

HOW TO BEAT THE BLUES

Try one of these simple ideas to cheer yourself up the next time you're feeling down.

• Call your best friend for a cheerful chat. Don't complain. Plan a great day out or a weekend treat instead.

• Watch your favorite funny movie.

• Keep a memory box full of happy things. Looking through old birthday cards, invitations, and favorite photographs will cheer you up.

• Put on your favorite music and dance away the blues.

• Pick some pretty flowers or interesting leaves and arrange them in a vase.

HOW TO GET RID OF KNOTS AND TANGLES

If your hair's really knotted, you'll need to take special care when you try to untangle it or you'll risk badly damaging your locks.

1. Start by smoothing lots of conditioner over your hair. If you don't have conditioner, olive oil is a good substitute.

2. Try to separate the strands using your fingers. Start at the ends of your hair and work up toward the roots. Keep going until you get out most of the large knots. Hold your hair near the scalp with one hand and use the other to untangle. That way, when you brush, there will be less pulling (and less pain).

3. Take a wide-tooth comb and work it gently through your hair from the bottom upward. Rub conditioner over the teeth of the comb to help it glide through your hair easily.

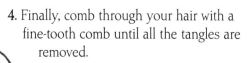

4. Finally, comb through your hair with a fine-tooth comb until all the tangles are removed.

5. Rinse out the conditioner once your hair is knot-free. Then shampoo and condition again.

Glamour Girl Tip: Do you wake up every morning with knotted hair? Try placing a silk scarf over your pillow. It'll keep your hair from becoming knotted while you sleep.

HOW TO FRENCH BRAID YOUR HAIR

A single braid that follows the curve of your head from the crown to the nape of your neck, a French braid is similar to a basic three-strand braid, except that you pick up extra strands of hair as you work your way down. As long as your hair is longer than chin-length, you should be able to manage it. Get together with a friend and practice on each other.

Here's how to do it:

1. Separate the hair from ear to ear across the top of your friend's head. Gather the top section and divide it into three equal strands as though you're making an ordinary braid.

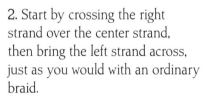

2. Start by crossing the right strand over the center strand, then bring the left strand across, just as you would with an ordinary braid.

3. Before you braid the third strand, scoop up an extra section of hair taken from the loose hair directly underneath it.

4. Continue braiding, but from now on, add an extra section of hair to each strand as you go. Try to take a similar amount of hair each time to keep the braid even.

5. The braid will naturally follow the curve of your friend's head as you pick up and include the new hair. Keep going until you reach the nape of her neck and all of the hair has been included.

6. Finish by braiding the rest of the hair to the end and secure it with a pretty hair elastic or ribbon.

HOW TO GET RID OF FLAKY LIPS

Cold weather can lead to sore, dry lips. Here's a great way to repair them and keep them soft and flake-free:

• Coat your lips with petroleum jelly.

• Leave it on for ten minutes to soften any hard flakes of skin.

• Cover your index finger with a damp washcloth and gently massage your lips. This will remove the petroleum jelly and the bits of dead skin at the same time.

• Rub a little petroleum jelly or lip balm onto your lips to keep the problem from happening again.

HOW TO HAVE THE BEST MANNERS

Use these helpful hints to have the best manners.

- No matter how hungry you are, it's still rude to cut the lunch line. As a general rule, there should be plenty of food to go around, so there's no rush.

- Losing can be difficult, but try not to sulk if you don't win every time. It can be just as hard not to be a gloating winner. Always remember to congratulate everyone else for playing well.

- Although it's tempting to jump right onto the bus or train, other travelers will appreciate it if you let them get off first.

- If you're trying to win an argument, you're much more likely to get positive results with cool reason rather than a hot temper.

- If a friend or relative is nice enough to give you a present, it's a good idea to have a polite response ready even if you don't like the gift. Say things like "Oh, I love it!," "I couldn't have thought of something so original," and "That'll be really useful." Always say "Thank you" and send a note as well.

If you can manage all of that, you are definitely a glamorous goddess!

HOW TO ORDER FOOD IN A RESTAURANT

If your family is going out for a special meal, remember these tips and you'll be able to order your food with style and ease:

- Don't be afraid to ask what something is if you are unsure. It's much better than getting a surprise on your plate.

- Some restaurants have hundreds of items on the menu, so don't bother to read the whole thing. Pick a section you like the look of and choose something from there.

- It's perfectly okay to order a drink first if you need more time to decide. Don't be rushed into ordering too soon.

- Take a peek at what people are eating at other tables. If they look as though they're enjoying their meal, choose the same dish.

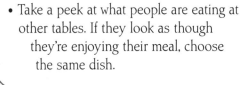

- Try not to order too much. There's nothing worse than overindulging and feeling terrible afterward.

- Be prepared to try something new – you just might enjoy it.

Bon appétit!

HOW TO HAVE A WHITER SMILE

Sparkling teeth and fresh breath are a
real beauty boost. These tips will help
you get the whitest smile possible.

- Brush your teeth twice a day
  to remove plaque. This is the
  sticky layer that builds up on
  teeth and it is the main cause
  of tooth decay.

- Brush for at least two minutes
  each time. Hum along to some
  music while you do it to help
  pass the time more quickly.

- Don't forget to brush your tongue as
  well as your teeth. This will clear the
  surface of old food and help prevent
  bad breath.

- An old toothbrush can't do its job properly, so change yours
  every three months or sooner if the bristles are damaged.

- Use dental floss regularly to clean between your teeth where
  your toothbrush can't reach.

- Visit your dentist twice a year to make sure your teeth are in
  perfect health.

- A natural remedy for sweeter-smelling breath is to chew
  parsley leaves. They're rich in a chemical called chlorophyll,
  which helps freshen breath.

- To help prevent tooth decay, limit your consumption of candy and other sugary foods and drinks.

- Keep your breath fresh by rinsing thoroughly with a mouthwash. You can make your own using a strong peppermint tea. Pour hot water over two tea bags and wait for it to cool before popping the cup in the fridge to chill.

- If you'd like really sparkling teeth, you can make your own whitening toothpaste. Baking soda has been used for years as a natural tooth whitener. It's really inexpensive and available in the supermarket. Dip a dampened toothbrush into the soda, then gently brush your teeth to remove any stains and improve whiteness.

HOW TO LOOK BEAUTIFUL FOR FREE

The best three beauty treats of all are actually free: sleep, fresh air, and lots of water.

- Breathing in fresh air literally oxygenates your skin so that it looks rosy and fresh.

- Most of us simply don't drink enough water. Two-thirds of our bodies are made up of water, so it's essential to replenish with six to eight glasses each day.

- As well as boosting your energy levels, sleep gives your body the chance to repair and renew itself so you look even more beautiful the next morning.

HOW TO MAKE YOUR OWN JEWELRY BOX

If you have lots of pretty bracelets, beads, and rings, you probably need somewhere special to keep them. It's easy to turn an old carton or container into your own decorated jewelry box.

What you'll need:

• An empty cardboard box (an old chocolate box is ideal)

• Various patterned papers to decorate with. Be as imaginative as you can. You could use pictures from old magazines and newspapers, old wrapping paper, used postage stamps, old musical scores, or glittery stickers.

• Clear-drying liquid craft glue

• Fabric to line the box (felt or velvet work well)

• Scissors

What to do:

1. Cut up your pieces of paper.

2. Glue the pieces of paper to the outside of the box, making sure they overlap. Keep going until the whole box is covered. If you want your box to look old, you can "age" the paper. While the glue is drying simply leave a tea bag in water for a few minutes, then brush the tea over the surface of the box and leave it to dry.

3. Brush a layer of glue all over the surface of the box. This will help protect the box and will make it look shinier.

4. Once the glue's dry on the outside, it's time to decorate the inside. Simply cut your chosen fabric to fit inside the base, sides, and lid of your box and glue into place.

5. When it's dry, fill your new jewelry box with your favorite trinkets.

HOW TO REMOVE INK STAINS FROM YOUR FINGERS

Oh, no! You have an important birthday party to attend, but your pen has leaked all over your hands. It's easy to bleach away the stains with an ordinary lemon. Just cut the lemon in half and rub the cut side over the ink stains. Wash your hands with gentle soap afterward, then rub on some hand cream.

HOW TO LOOK (AND FEEL) PERKY WHEN YOU'RE FEELING TIRED

When you've got a busy day ahead but you wake up feeling exhausted, here's how to perk yourself up:

• Freshen up with a tingly lemon shower gel. If you can bear it, switch the water to cold just before you finish showering for an ultrainvigorating start to your day.

• Wash your hair while you're in the shower. Take the time to massage your scalp with your fingertips. It's a great pick-me-up.

• Eat some breakfast. It really is the most important meal of the day, and it will give you the energy you need to get going. Try whole wheat toast and a glass of orange juice, or a bowl of granola with a chopped banana and yogurt.

• Try this simple deep-breathing exercise to increase your energy level. Lie on your back, supporting your head with a cushion, and place your hands on your tummy. Shut your eyes and concentrate on expanding your tummy as you breathe in, and flattening it as you breathe out. Continue for five minutes.

• Your body needs lots of fresh air and daylight, so take a brisk ten-minute walk at some point in the day and drink plenty of water to refresh you.

• Spritz yourself with a fresh-smelling body spray. It will lift your spirits and make you smell great, too.

• Gently pinch your cheeks to give them a red glow that will make your look instantly healthier.

- Lie down and place a cold tea bag over each eye for five minutes. Tea contains tannin, which reduces puffiness around your eyes and makes them look brighter.

HOW TO GIVE YOURSELF A FACE MASSAGE

Just like every part of your body, your face will look better after a mini massage.

1. Pour a few drops of olive oil into your hands and smooth it onto your face and neck.

2. Use your fingers to stroke upward from the base of your neck to your chin.

3. Now stroke up one side of your face, then the other.

4. Go around your nose and up toward your forehead.

5. Stroke across your forehead from left to right, using one hand.

6. Finish off by gently drawing a circle around each eye using one finger.

HOW TO DO A FRENCH MANICURE

When it comes to nail trends, there's one look that never goes out of fashion – the French manicure. It leaves your nails looking clean, fresh, and healthy, and it matches any outfit.

Here's how to do it:

1. The classic French manicure uses two coats of pale pink polish. Look for a natural shade without any extra sparkles.

2. The best way to apply nail polish is in three strokes – one down the center of the nail and one stroke on either side. Apply two coats, giving each one plenty of time to dry.

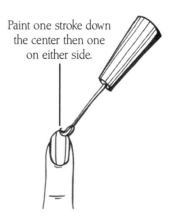

Paint one stroke down the center then one on either side.

Glamour Girl Tip: To turn a French manicure into an American manicure, use a beige polish instead of a pink one.

3. Now it's time to paint the tips of your nails with a white polish. Be careful not to overload the brush or the polish will flow down the bristles too quickly for you to control.

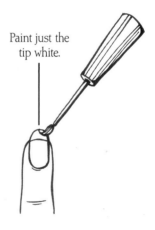

Paint just the tip white.

Glamour Girl Tip: Rest your hand on a firm surface to keep your hands steady and create a perfect finish.

4. Once the white tips of your nails are dry, paint on a clear topcoat of polish to seal the color and create a chip-free finish.

Glamour Girl Tip: If you're feeling impatient, you can dry nail polish more quickly by blasting your nails with a cold jet of air from your hair dryer.

HOW TO LOOK YOUR BEST IN A PHOTOGRAPH

Make the most of any opportunity you get in front of a camera. Practice these useful pointers to make sure you always look your best.

• Brush your hair quickly in case it's sticking up and check that you don't have anything stuck between your teeth.

• Don't face the camera head-on. Turn your body slightly to one side, but keep your head facing forward for a more natural pose.

• Don't look directly into the lens. Instead, look slightly to the side. This will help you to avoid red eye.

• Press your tongue to the roof of your mouth, lift your chin slightly as though you are stretching to look over a high garden fence and smile. This way you'll avoid any unflattering shadows under your chin.

• If your photographer is using a flash, widen your eyes a little just before the picture is taken so that you're not caught with your eyes closed.

• Try not to stand with your back to a light, as it will make you appear in silhouette.

• People always look good in a photograph when they are laughing. Try to think of something funny just before the shot and you'll be caught at your best possible moment.

HOW TO MAKE AN ACCEPTANCE SPEECH

You've finally been nominated for an award and, suddenly, out of all the nominees, the host announces that you're the winner! You have a limited time to make a dazzling acceptance speech, so make sure yours is the one that people are talking about the next day. Follow these pointers to make the most of your moment at the mic:

• If possible, choose a fun way to get onto the stage. Run across the seats, do cartwheels, crowd-surf, or dance – anything, as long as you make a lasting impression.

• Remember to mention that it's an honor to be singled-out from such a wonderful group of nominees.

• Tears are fine, but make sure everyone can still hear you.

• Memorize a short list of the most important people to thank and then say "Everyone else – you know who you are."

• When the music starts playing, leave the stage immediately.

Glamour Girl Tip: If you don't win, remember to plaster a delighted-looking smile on your face and applaud loudly until everyone stops looking.

HOW TO MAKE RAIN BOOTS STYLISH

Rain boots might seem like a fashion no-no, but with a little creativity you'll be able to easily carry off a long walk through a storm. These tips are guaranteed to help you stay stylish in the country or the city.

• Choose a pair of trendy boots with a cute design like funky flowers or rainbows. Even celebrities wear colorful boots to brighten up their winter outfits and keep their feet dry.

• Alternatively, you could funk up your old boots by using waterproof pens or acrylic paints.

• Always try to match your outfit to your boots. If you can coordinate with extra accessories, even better.

Now even on the dullest day you'll be able to stay stylish and make the most boring rain boots a fashion must-have.

HOW TO GIVE
A GREAT INTERVIEW

If you're about to give an interview to a magazine or TV journalist, it's important to prepare in advance. Good tactics can make a big difference and help you to leave a great lasting impression.

- When you meet the interviewer, order a cool drink, such as a lemonade or iced tea, to keep your throat from getting dry. It will also come in handy if you are asked any difficult questions. Take a long sip of your drink while you come up with a good answer.

- Don't forget to look the interviewer right in the eye when you meet him or her. Shake the interviewer's hand firmly and smile confidently so he or she will know how friendly and open you are.

- Name-dropping can be impressive. Mention your favorite celebrities by their first names to convince the interviewer that you're the best of friends.

- If you're about to appear in your school play or sing in a talent contest, bring it up as often as you dare. The more publicity you can get, the better.

- People will soon get bored of hearing about you if you give hundreds of interviews. Pick only your favorite magazine or TV show to talk to and give them an exclusive instead.

- Make sure everyone knows how to spell your name correctly.

HOW TO MAKE YOUR OWN PERFUME

This is a simple recipe for making perfume at home. Just use your favorite garden flowers.

What you'll need:

- 1 cup of water
- 1 cup of fresh flower petals, chopped
- Muslin square (a clean cotton dishcloth will work, too)
- Bowl and saucepan
- Pretty bottle

What to do:

1. Spread the muslin in the bowl, letting the edges hang over the rim.

2. Fill with the flower petals and cover them with water.

3. Cover with a plate and let stand overnight.

4. The next day, carefully lift the muslin cloth out of the bowl and squeeze the scented water into a saucepan.

5. Get an adult to help you gently heat the scented water until only about ¼ cup remains.

6. Leave to cool, then pour into your pretty bottle.

7. Dab on your perfume and smell gorgeous. Kept in the fridge, this perfume should last for up to a month.

HOW TO BLOW-DRY YOUR HAIR PERFECTLY

Keep your hair looking sleek and shiny with a salon-style blow-dry at home. This step-by-step guide will help you get it right.

1. Comb your hair gently after shampooing and conditioning to remove any knots. (See page 78 if your hair's really tangled.)

2. Gently squeeze your hair to remove any excess water.

3. Wrap your hair up in a towel for five minutes.

4. Get to work with your hair dryer. Make sure you blow-dry down the length of your hair from the roots to the tips. This makes the outer cuticle of each strand lie flat, which means shinier hair.

5. Work the hair dryer quickly over your head, ruffling your hair with your fingers at the same time.

6. Tip your head upside down while you direct the dryer's nozzle at the roots. This will build body in your hair.

7. When your hair is just beginning to feel dry, start using a brush to style it.

8. Style the front of your hair first, as it's the part everyone will notice. Work your way around to the sides and back. It may be helpful to use clips to section off the parts of your hair you're not working on.

9. Give your hair a final blast of cool air to set it.

10. Ruffle your hair with your fingers to add a little texture.

HOW TO SMELL SWEET

Nothing says glamour like smelling great. Try out these tactics and you'll always be the sweetest-smelling girl around.

FRESH AS A DAISY

It goes without saying, but you should have a bath or shower every single day.

HERBAL REMEDY

Add sprigs of herbs to your bath for a natural treat. Refreshing ones to try are mint, rosemary, and thyme. Either raid the

THE GIRLS' BOOK OF GLAMOUR

kitchen cupboard for dried ones or check out the garden for
fresh herbs. Once the tub is full, toss in the herbs and let them
float in the water to release their scent.

FULL STEAM AHEAD

Adding a few drops of perfume to the floor of the shower will
create beautifully scented steam.

A FRESH START

Sprinkle a dry towel with your favorite fresh fragrance. Put it in
the clothes dryer for a few minutes until it heats up and give
yourself a vigorous rubdown. The hot fragranced towel will make
you feel fabulously awake and alert.

SWEET DREAMS

Sprinkle your bedsheets with scented talcum powder! You'll
wake up smelling lovely.

EAT THAI

Smell sweet with Thai food. Believe it or not, this type of
food is said to produce the nicest body smells, so take the
opportunity to eat lots of it! It contains plenty of aromatic
ingredients, such as mint, lemongrass, and coconut. Go easy
on the garlic, though!

LAYERS OF LOVELINESS

Learn to layer fragrances to smell beautiful all day. Start with a
scented bath oil and soap. Move on to body lotion and finish
with a light splash of perfume.

HOW TO TIE-DYE A T-SHIRT

The best way to brighten up a boring old white T-shirt is by tie-dyeing it. It's much easier than it looks to create a groovy sunburst design and add some hippy chic to your wardrobe.

What you'll need:

- A pack of cold-water dye in any color you like
- Salt
- Metal spoon
- Rubber bands
- Rubber gloves
- Jug filled with cold water
- Large bucket or container filled with warm water
- White T-shirt

Glamour Girl Tip: Check that it's okay to use things from the kitchen before you start, or buy your own set especially for dyeing.

Here's how:

1. Prepare the mixture. Open the dye container and pour the powder into the jug of cold water. Let it dissolve.

2. Follow the directions on the package of dye and add the required amount of salt. (Every

99

brand of dye is slightly different, so read the instructions carefully.) Stir until everything's dissolved.

3. Pour the dye mixture into the bowl of warm water. Stir again until thoroughly mixed.

4. To prepare the T-shirt, pinch the fabric in the middle of the front. Securely twist a rubber band around the pinch. The sections of fabric covered by the rubber band won't absorb the dye and will remain white.

5. Next, bunch the fabric together and tie a second rubber band around the pinch about 2 inches from the first.

6. Continue adding rubber bands, 2 inches apart, until the front of the T-shirt is completely wrapped.

7. If you like, repeat the same process again on the back and the sleeves of the T-shirt.

8. Immerse your T-shirt in the bowl of dye. Push it down into the liquid with the spoon to make sure it's thoroughly wet.

9. Leave your T-shirt to soak for an hour, then squeeze out the water and rinse away any excess dye.

10. Hang the T-shirt up on a line to dry, then remove the rubber bands. *Voilà!* You now have a beautiful sunburst T-shirt.

HOW TO SOOTHE TIRED FEET

It's no surprise that at the end of a hard day at school (or at the mall) your feet can feel tired and sore. Try this quick and simple remedy to bring them back to life.

Soak your feet for five minutes in a bowl of warm water to which you've added a handful of sea salt. Then lie down on your back on the floor with your feet up, resting them on the edge of the sofa. Stay there for ten minutes.

HOW TO MAKE A DOOR CURTAIN

Create a glamorous entrance to your bedroom with a beaded door curtain. It looks fabulous and is easy to make.

What you'll need:

- Thick piece of ribbon cut to the same width as your doorframe
- About 30 plastic straws in any color
- 12 pieces of fishing line or strong clear thread, each 6 feet long
- Around 200 plastic beads
- A few thumbtacks to secure the curtain to your doorframe
- Scissors

How to make it:

1. Lay the thick piece of ribbon on the floor. Secure each strand of fishing line to the ribbon at equal intervals. Do this by looping one end of the thread over the ribbon and tying a knot.

2. Cut the straws into 2-inch pieces.

3. String the beads and straw pieces onto each length of fishing line, alternating them and finishing with a bead.

4. When the fishing line is full, feed the end of the thread through the last bead twice and finish with a knot to secure it in place.

5. Repeat for each piece of fishing line.

6. Get an adult to hang the curtain over your door with thumbtacks.

HOW TO LIP-SYNCH SUCCESSFULLY

If you don't have a good singing voice but want to become a pop star, it's important to learn how to lip-synch. This is a kind of miming where you look as if you're singing a song even though you're not. Here are some tips to help you:

• Choose a simple song that you can really put your heart and soul into. Look for one that is funny, very emotional, or has a strong beat.

• Learn the lyrics! There's nothing worse than forgetting the words mid-performance.

• Really think about what the words of the song mean and aim to express this with your body language during your show.

• Don't be afraid to exaggerate your facial movements during your performance. The audience will really enjoy it.

• Dress up! It will really boost your confidence.

- Never turn your back on your audience. It will make it more difficult to keep their attention.

- Don't worry if you think people suspect you're lip-synching. Some of the most famous singers do it. Concentrate on performing as well as you can.

- If you're not confident enough to perform alone, get a friend or a group of friends to join you. There are plenty of duets and songs by bands to choose from.

HOW TO BE THE COOLEST PARTY GUEST

Follow these simple rules to be the hippest girl at the party!

- Always be fashionably late – twenty minutes or so is ideal. Don't be too late, though, as you don't want to appear rude.

- Smile and look around at everyone when you enter a room, even if you don't know anyone. It will make people want to come talk to you.

- Mingle with as many people as possible. Next time people will notice if you're not there and you'll probably end up with even more party invitations!

- Don't be the last to leave. Even the best party girl has to get enough beauty sleep!

HOW TO MAKE A BUTTON-AND-BEAD CHARM BRACELET

What you'll need:

- A selection of pretty buttons (Ask an adult if you can raid his or her sewing box for some, snip them off old, unwanted clothes, or scour thrift stores and sewing stores for bargains.)

- A selection of pretty beads

- Elastic thread

- Sewing thread cut into 4-inch lengths.

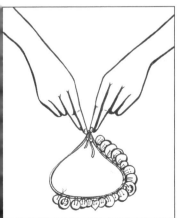

What to do:

1. Measure enough elastic to fit around your wrist and then add on 3 inches. Knot the ends together and snip away any excess elastic.

2. Take one bead or button at a time, and feed a length of sewing thread through its hole. Then secure it on the thread with a knot.

3. Now tie the button or bead around the elastic. Secure with a double knot and snip off the excess thread.

4. Keep on adding buttons and beads until you can't see the elastic anymore.

Glamour Girl Tip: Cram as many buttons and beads onto the elastic as you can. The more they overlap, the better the bracelet will look.

HOW TO LOOK INSTANTLY TALLER

Good posture is the best way to add inches to your height. It'll make you look more confident, too. Look in a mirror and check yourself out.

- DO keep your neck straight from your hairline to your shoulders.

- DON'T let your head hang forward.

- DO keep your chest high and your shoulder blades flat.

- DON'T hunch up your shoulders or slump forward.

- DO stand tall with a shallow curve in the small of your back.

- DON'T stick your tummy out.

- DO tuck your backside in.

- DON'T stand with your feet turned out. Keep them parallel with each other.

HOW TO WRITE YOUR FIRST AUTOBIOGRAPHY

An autobiography is a story that you write all about yourself and your life. It is a great way to tell fans how you became famous, so it is a good idea to start taking notes now.

- Keep a journal. When you look back, you'll be able to remember exactly how you were feeling each day and use it to add lots of emotional touches and details to your story.

- Read the autobiography of someone you admire for inspiration.

- Ask your family and friends for any funny anecdotes they can remember about your early years. These are especially good if they show how talented you were, even as a baby.

- Remember to be totally honest. It's almost certain that someone will know if you have exaggerated anything, which could lead to embarrassment later on.

HOW TO PRETEND YOU CAN DANCE FLAMENCO

Fool people that you can dance the flamenco with this mini-routine. Get your friends to clap their hands rhythmically while you perform these moves as dramatically as you can.

1. Stand as tall as you can. Reach up with your right arm and pretend you're plucking an apple from a high branch of a tree. Hold the imaginary apple with the very tips of your fingers.

2. Now pretend you are going to take a bite from the apple. Rotate your wrist clockwise as you bend your elbow and bring your imaginary apple toward your mouth (don't actually bite).

3. Now start swinging your hips, stomping your feet, and turning in circles.

4. Pretend to throw the apple to the ground, a look of utter disgust on your face.

5. Now stamp on the imaginary apple, moving your feet faster and faster as you crush it to a pulp.

6. Repeat.

HOW TO EAT SPAGHETTI

Forget about cutting up your spaghetti or fiddling with spoons. All you need is a fork and a little know-how.

1. Poke the prongs of the fork into the spaghetti and scoop up a small amount. Lift it high off the plate to release it from the rest of the spaghetti and to allow any stray strands to fall. If you've taken too much, now's the time to wiggle the fork slightly and let some excess fall off.

2. Look for an area of the plate that's food-free. Quickly point the prongs of the fork straight down onto it.

3. Twirl the fork a few times to create a roll of strands.

4. Quickly flick your wrist and place the rolled-up spaghetti into your mouth. *Bravo!*

HOW TO DRESS TO SUIT YOUR ZODIAC SIGN

Each sign of the zodiac is said to have its own special fashion style. Check out the looks linked to your sign and see if it sounds like you.

ARIES (MARCH 21 TO APRIL 20)

You're a trendsetter who is always willing to try new looks. You've got brilliant fashion radar and you know whether an outfit's going to become a hit or a miss. Your favorite colors are red and black.

TAURUS (APRIL 21 TO MAY 21)

You'd prefer a vintage cashmere sweater over a cheap T-shirt from the mall. You love subtle, expensive shades of brown, khaki, and cream.

GEMINI (MAY 22 TO JUNE 21)

You get bored hanging on to any outfit for too long. You mix and match styles and love shimmery fabrics and colored patterns.

CANCER (JUNE 22 TO JULY 23)

You love comfortable, feminine clothes like soft sweaters and floaty skirts. If you find a piece of clothing you like, you keep it in your wardrobe for years. You love to dress in soft blues and greens.

LEO (JULY 24 TO AUGUST 23)

You wear anything that makes a statement, from flowing tops to cropped jackets. You love gold, red, bronze, and orange.

VIRGO (AUGUST 24 TO SEPTEMBER 23)

Virgo is the best-dressed zodiac sign of all. You spend a lot of time taking care of your clothes. You love neat and tidy looks and soft fabrics in natural colors like green, gray, and brown.

LIBRA (SEPTEMBER 24 TO OCTOBER 23)

You have great taste and prefer classic looks. Somehow, though, you always manage to put an outfit together that looks up-to-date and modern. You opt for rich blues, dark pinks, and black.

SCORPIO (OCTOBER 24 TO NOVEMBER 22)

One day your style is classic and preppy, the next day your style is barefoot and natural. The colors you keep coming back to are black and red.

SAGITTARIUS (NOVEMBER 23 TO DECEMBER 21)

You love colorful, casual clothes that let you move, and you don't really care what others think of your look. You prefer soft, natural fabrics in earthy shades of purple, green, and dark blue.

CAPRICORN (DECEMBER 22 TO JANUARY 20)

You're not a label snob. As long as you like an outfit, you don't care how much it costs or what store it comes from. Color-wise, you favor charcoal gray, brown, and black.

AQUARIUS (JANUARY 21 TO FEBRUARY 19)

You're unconventional with clothes and your friends often look to you for a hint of what style might be in next. You experiment with color but always find yourself coming back to shades of blue.

PISCES (FEBRUARY 20 TO MARCH 20)

You would happily buy all of your clothes from a thrift store, but when you dress up you can look as good as anyone. Your favorite colors are silver, purple, and cream.

HOW TO WALK IN HIGH-HEELED SHOES

High-heeled shoes look lovely if you're off to a party or a wedding, but they can be difficult to walk in at first. Follow this simple guide and you'll soon be skipping around like a real lady.

- If you're not used to heels, choose a low heel or a wedge (where the space between the heel and toe is filled in) to start with. Then you can move up to taller heels once you've had a chance to practice.

- Find a good place to practice where you have plenty to hold on to and stand up slowly and carefully. Your center of gravity will be higher than usual, so flex each knee a little to steady yourself.

- Keep your backside tucked in and balance on the balls of your feet. Take a few steps forward, placing each heel first before putting your toe down. Be careful not to get a heel caught in the carpet.

- Keep practicing at home for a couple of days until you feel ready to go out. Try a short trip around the corner and back before attempting a longer outing. Soon you'll be able to run for a bus with ease.

Glamour Girl Tip: Take a spare pair of flat shoes along, too, just in case you get tired.

HOW TO FIND THE PERFECT PERFUME

There are thousands of perfumes on the market, which means it can be hard to find the one you really like and which most suits your personality.

TRIAL AND ERROR

• Head for the perfume counter at a department store or a large pharmacy for the best choice. Try a maximum of three scents. After that, your nose will get tired and they will all start to smell the same.

• Start by taking a look at the ingredients before you spray. If you're very girly, you might love floral perfumes. If you're sporty, citrus scents like lemon or grapefruit could be ideal.

• Spray a little onto the inside of your wrist or elbow, then wait ten minutes for the perfume to develop properly. You shouldn't buy a perfume even if you like it right away. Perfumes often smell quite different after a couple of hours. If you like the way it smells on your skin later on in the day, you'll know you've found a scent you really like.

HOW TO WEAR IT

The best place to wear a perfume is on one of your pulse points, which is where the blood is closest to your skin's surface. These include your temples, the side of your neck (not behind your ears!), in the crook of your elbow, your inner wrists, the backs of your knees and on the front of your ankles. You can also spray freshly washed hair so that you waft a delicious scent around you as you move your head.

HOW TO MAKE A
MOOD BOARD

The most glamorous girls always know what suits them, as well as the styles and colors they really love. You can work out your own personal style, too, by creating a Mood Board for your bedroom.

First, you'll need a bulletin board for the wall. If you don't have one of these, try securing four cork floor tiles to your wall with Sticky Tac.

Start collecting clippings from fashion magazines, photos, old postcards, advertisements, paint swatches, fabric scraps, leaves, or anything at all. The only important thing is that you really love everything. Take your time deciding which things really appeal to you. Spread them out on your bed while you decide. You may be able to gather them into little sections of similar colors or style.

Once you're happy with your selection, arrange them on your bulletin board. Now sit back and take a look – your personal taste will be there for you to admire whenever you want.

HOW TO SEEM CONFIDENT WHEN YOU'RE NOT

The next time you're feeling shy and overwhelmed, try out these DOs and DON'Ts to make others think you're feeling completely confident (even if you're not)!

- DON'T wear dull colors.
  Instead of trying to blend in with the background, get yourself noticed by wearing confident reds, oranges, or yellows.

- DO get your body language right.
  Hold your head high no matter how nervous you feel. Don't clasp your hands in front of you or fold them. It's much better to stand with your arms hanging relaxed at your sides. Sit with your hands resting loosely in your lap.

- DON'T hide behind your hair.
  Let people see your face. Hair swept back into a neat ponytail says that you're okay about people looking at you.

- DO smile.
  People often confuse shyness with unfriendliness. A smile shows you're friendly and makes people feel relaxed around you.

- DON'T talk too quickly.
  Relax and take a deep breath. Take your time and give yourself a chance to think about what you want to say. Avoid just blurting out the first thing that comes into your head.

- DO look people in the eye.
  One of the most obvious signs of shyness is when you avoid making eye contact with the person you're talking to.

- DON'T chew your nails.
  Nibbling on fingers is a dead giveaway that you're feeling nervous.

- DO lift your spirits with a scent.
  Apply a dot of grapefruit or another citrus essential oil on your wrists before heading out the door in the morning. Both are uplifting scents that are great for boosting your confidence.

HOW TO STRIKE A POSE

When everyone is looking your way, it's vital to make sure that your every move seems as naturally glamorous as possible, whether you're just picking something up at the corner store or you're heading out for a night on the town. Next time you're in the spotlight, try out these moves.

THE HAIR FLIP

As you step onto the school bus, smile, wave, and flip your head up so that your hair swishes out behind you.

THE LOOK BEHIND YOU

Walk past your waiting photographers without stopping. Just when they think you've ignored them, completely stop, put one hand on your hip, and look back over your shoulder before giving them your best smile.

THE BIG TRIP

It's best to avoid this one, but it's important to be prepared, just in case you should trip and fall. Always laugh it off and gracefully get on your feet again as quickly as possible.

HOW TO EMPHASIZE YOUR EYE COLOR

A great way to make your natural eye color really stand out at parties is to wear clothes in just the right shade. Forget about wearing blues if you have blue eyes, and browns if you have brown eyes. These are the best choices:

Eye Color: pale blue
Try: lilac or pastel pink

Eye Color: mid-to-dark blue
Try: peach or gold

Eye Color: light brown
Try: honey brown or khaki green

Eye Color: dark brown
Try: caramel brown or olive green

Eye Color: pale green
Try: lavender or blue-gray

Eye Color: dark green
Try: peach or plum

Eye Color: hazel
Try: moss green or purple

HOW TO BEAD YOUR HAIR

Beaded hair looks really pretty and costs just pennies. It only takes a little time and practice to achieve.

You'll need:

- A handful of beads with large holes. Plastic ones are best as they're lighter. (You don't want to be too weighed down!)

- A spool of colored thread

How to do it:

1. Pick up a strand of hair about the thickness of a shoelace.

2. Divide it into three smaller strands.

3. Braid the three strands together until you have about 2 inches of hair left at the ends.

4. Wet the end of the braid and smooth the ends together.

5. Thread a bead through your hair and push it up onto the braid.

6. Add as many beads as you like, carefully pushing each one up the braid.

7. When you've finished, wind a length of

thread around the end of the braid and tie it in place. You can also use a small, thin hair elastic if you prefer.

8. Repeat the whole process to make as many braids as you like. You can even enlist some friends to help you bead all of your hair.

HOW TO TELL WHAT THE SHAPE OF YOUR LIPSTICK MEANS

Raid your friends' makeup bags, whip out their used lipsticks or lip balms, and explain how the shape of the tip reveals loads about their personalities.

FLAT TOP

You're dependable and serious. You care what people think about you.

CONCAVE TOP

This bowl-shape means you're friendly, exciting, and love a dare.

SLANTED TOP

If the end is close to its original shape, you probably stick to the rules and don't like too much attention.

ROUNDED TOP

You're a lovable, friendly person who enjoys being busy.

POINTED TOP

You're kind and easygoing and can be relied on in a crisis.

HOW TO TAKE CARE OF YOUR SKIN IN THE SUMMER

Everyone loves a day at the beach in the summer, but no one likes getting burned by the sun. Check out this safe sun plan.

- Apply sunscreen (SPF 15 or higher) first thing in the morning before getting dressed so you won't miss any areas.

- Lips are especially prone to burning and chapping in the sun, so put on some lip balm with an SPF of 15 or higher.

- Stay in the shade between 12 noon and 3 o'clock when the sun is hottest. Or, cover up with a T-shirt and a hat.

- If you like to swim, choose a waterproof sunscreen and be sure to reapply it when you get out of the water.

HOW TO TAKE CARE OF YOUR SKIN IN THE WINTER

- Chilly temperatures and cold winds can make your skin dry and itchy. Always protect yourself with warm mittens, a cozy scarf, and a cute hat.

- Dress in layers that will keep you warm from head to toe. Light cotton or a thin synthetic fabric next to your skin helps keep you warm and dry.

- Bathe or shower in lukewarm water. Hot baths may sound nice, but the heat can dry out the natural oils in your skin and make it even itchier than before.

- Don't lick sore lips to try to soothe them – you'll just make them even flakier. Put on some lip balm or petroleum jelly instead.

HOW TO ESCAPE A CROWD OF FANS

It's difficult to be polite and glamorous all the time. If you just need some time to yourself, use these top tips to get away from the crowds.

- Dress up in a disguise. A wig and dark glasses are a great idea, but don't go overboard. A wooden leg and a parrot will only draw more attention to you.

- Get to know your route home like the back of your hand. Try to plan a detour and give everyone the slip when they least expect it.

- Perfect your celebrity-style wave. It's best performed when getting into an expensive car, but the school bus will do in a pinch. Walk quickly with your head down. Just before you get in, stop and turn to face your fans. Raise your arm briefly and flash a quick smile. Remember – the more excited your fans are, the more disinterested your wave should be. Now turn and enter the bus, refusing all autographs.

- Come up with a false name – the name of your favorite cartoon combined with your first pet is a simple way of doing this. Use it whenever you travel to avoid detection.

- If you find your exit blocked by autograph-hunters at your local café, politely ask the owner if you can go through the kitchen instead and leave through the back door.

HOW TO TAKE CHARGE OF OUT-OF-CONTROL HAIR

The weather can wreak havoc on your hair. If your pretty curls are always frizzy, or flyaway static is ruining your lovely tresses, try these helpful hints:

Frizzy hair:

- Use a conditioner each time you wash your hair to keep it as sleek as possible. Save lots of time with a spray-on and leave-in brand.

- Use your fingers as styling tools instead of brushes and combs. You're less likely to create frizz this way.

- Rub a few drops of almond oil between your palms, then smooth over your hair to soothe crazy curls.

Flyaway hair:

- Dry winter air can literally make your hair stand on end. Use a wooden brush to help reduce static electricity.

- Use a moisturizing shampoo and conditioner to prevent your hair from drying out.

- Spritz antistatic hairspray onto your brush before styling your hair.

HOW TO CHOOSE THE RIGHT SUNGLASSES FOR YOUR FACE SHAPE

Choosing the right pair of shades to suit your face shape can transform your whole look and give you just the right finishing touch. Check out how to figure out your face shape on page 40, then decide which frames would suit you the best.

ROUND-SHAPED FACE

Look for broad styles that are equal to the width of your face. Square lenses look good, too.

HEART-SHAPED FACE

Delicate or rimless frames suit your pretty face shape perfectly. Angular shapes are also a good choice for you.

SQUARE-SHAPED FACE

Soft, gently curved oval-shaped frames soften your defined features perfectly.

OVAL-SHAPED FACE

It's your lucky day! Any frame style or shape is good for an oval face.

HOW TO BE A GODDESS

Now that you have achieved goddesslike status by reading this book, you'll need to learn how to cope with the stresses and strains this role may bring.

• If you really want to look like a goddess, borrow an old white sheet and drape it around yourself in the style of a Roman toga.

• Wind some pretty flowers through your hair. Always remember to leave a trail of blossoms wherever you walk.

• Smile gently at all times to give people the impression that you're calm and serene.

• If people are nice enough to offer you gifts, do your best to accept them with good manners and a sincere "thank you."

• One of the best goddess skills you will learn is wisdom. Use it well and try to give the best advice you can.

• Most importantly, never abuse your powers.